AF481843

Introduction

- ## What you will learn?

>> You will learn a basic and intermediate knowledge about what advertising is, how it does work, how it plays a vital role in consumer's minds etc.

- ## Who is this book for?

>> This book is mainly for those people interested in Advertising & Marketing (MBA Grads, Business Corporates, Non Fictions lovers etc.) or the people who wants to make career in Advertising industry.

- ## What is the purpose of the book?

>> The main purpose of the book is to let the interested people knows about the insights of Advertising and its digital trend in current world.

Contents

ADS MATTERS!

(A Proper Guide for the Beginners in Advertising)

The tactics and procedures used to bring items, services, ideas, or causes to the public's attention with the goal of convincing the public to respond in a specific way to what is marketed are referred to as advertising.

While most advertisements promote a product for sale, similar techniques are used to persuade people to drive carefully, donate to various organisations, or vote for political candidates, to name a few examples. In many countries, advertising is the primary source of revenue for the media (such as newspapers, magazines, or television stations) through which it is carried out. Advertising has grown into a major and vital service business in the non-communist world.

Characteristics Of Advertising

Paid Form: Advertising requires the advertiser (also referred to as sponsor) to acquire the creation of an advertising message, the acquisition of an advertising media slot, and therefore the monitoring of advertising efforts.

Promotional Tool: Advertising could be a component of a company's marketing mix.

One-Way Communication: Advertising could be a style of one-way communication within which firms connect with customers via various means.

Personal or Non-Personal Advertising: Advertising will be non-personal, like on TV, radio, or in newspapers, or extremely personal, like on social media and other cookie-based ads.

Goals/Objectives of Advertising

Advertising has three major goals:

To inform consumers about a brand or service, convince them to buy or execute a job, and to recall and reinforce the brand message.

In order to educate advertisements are used to raise brand recognition and exposure in a particular market. The first step in achieving company objectives is to educate potential clients about the brand and its goods.

Persuade Consumers to Complete a Specific Activity One of the most important goals of advertising is to persuade customers to perform a specific task. The activities might include purchasing or testing the items and services on offer, developing a brand image, and developing a favourable attitude toward the brand, among other things.

To recollect

Another goal of advertising is to reinforce the brand message and reassure current and prospective customers of the company's goals. Advertising assists the company in maintaining top-of-mind recognition and preventing clients from being stolen by competitors. This also aids in word-of-mouth advertising.

Why is advertising so important?

To the Clients

• **Convenience**: Targeted informational marketing help customers make better decisions by letting them know what best fits their needs and budget.

• **Customer awareness**: Advertising informs clients about the many items on the market and their features. Customers may use this information to compare items and select the best option for them.

• **Higher Quality**: Brands are the only ones that promote themselves and their products. Unbranded items do not have any ads. No firm wants to waste money on deceptive advertising, thus this assures greater quality for customers.

To The Industry

• **Brand and product awareness**: Advertising raises brand and product awareness among the target market.

• **Brand Image**: In the eyes of customers, clever advertising assists the firm in forming the ideal brand image and brand personality.

• **Product Differentiation**: Advertising aids in the differentiation of a company's product from that of rivals, as well as the communication of its characteristics and benefits to the target audience.

• **Increases Consumer Goodwill**: Advertising reinforces the brand's mission while also increasing customer goodwill.

• **Cost Effectiveness**: When compared to other parts of the marketing mix, advertising provides the message to a large audience at a low cost.

Advertising's Benefits

• **Lowers Per-Unit Cost**: The widespread attractiveness of ads raises demand for the product, benefiting the organisation by leveraging economies of scale.

• **Assists in Brand Building**: Advertisements are beneficial in promoting a company's brand. Advertised brands are favoured over those that do not.

• **Assists with the Launch of New Products**: When a new product is backed by advertising, it is much easier to launch it.

• **Increases Existing Customers' Confidence In The Brand**: Advertisements increase existing customers' trust in the brand because they feel proud when they see an advertising for the product or brand they use.

• **Aids in Customer Turnover Reduction**: Strategic advertising for new offerings and better service aids in customer turnover reduction.

• **Attracts New Consumers**: Attractive ads aid in the acquisition of new customers and the expansion of a firm.

Disadvantages of Advertising

• **Increases Costs**: Advertising is a commercial expense that is added to the product's cost. The end user is ultimately responsible for this expenditure.

• **Confuses the Consumer**: Too many commercials with identical promises might make it difficult for the buyer to decide what to buy and whether or not to buy the goods.It Can Be Misleading: Some commercials employ clever tactics to deceive buyers.

Why Advertising Is Only For Big Firms: Advertising is an expensive endeavour that only big businesses can afford. As a result, small enterprises are no longer in competition with large corporations, which gain a market monopoly.

• **Encourages the Sale of Substandard Items**: Effective advertising can lead to the sale of substandard products that are harmful to consumers.

Psychology in Advertising

5000. Every day, the average consumer is exposed to this amount of advertising. "How the hell can I get people to see my advertisements?" you're undoubtedly wondering.

Advertisers have known for a long time that they can use psychology to figure out what draws attention, leaves an impression, persuades, and leads to a buy. Having said that, you may employ psychology to ensure that your advertisement is effective.

Okay, that's fantastic. But how do you do it?

Continue scrolling if you want to understand how to make your adverts truly work, by which I mean get people to buy your goods.

Because you probably concentrate in marketing rather than psychology, this subject may be a little... hazy for you.

So, what is Advertising Psychology?

Psychology is the study of human nature, the psyche, and why individuals behave in certain ways.

Advertising is the art of persuading people to make particular purchases based on their behaviour. It's unsurprising that these two fields collide.

Psychology is the study of human nature, the psyche, and why individuals behave in certain ways.

A simple advertising needs a great deal of thinking and technique, as well as more planning than one might think. Each element of an advertisement, from the colour scheme and images to the actual words utilised, is meant to appeal to the customer in a unique way. Every feature is precisely designed to elicit a desired feeling or response utilising fundamental

Psychological concepts. While there are other psychological aspects to consider, emotions, persuasion and authority, memories, and colours are a few of the most frequent.

Emotions

Consumers' emotions are frequently exploited in advertising. Consumer desires and responses can be influenced by fear, love, pleasure, or vanity. Each of these emotions may be influenced and utilised to influence behaviour in different ways:

• Fear is a strong emotion that can be used as a motivator. Fear is a primal instinct, and nothing makes people feel more uneasy than being afraid. Fear tactics can be used in advertising to create an uncomfortable position or situation, then offer a solution in the form of a product or service. "The fear of missing out" is one approach that uses fear. Phrases like "one day only," "limited time only," and "only a few left" are used to identify this approach. These "calls to action" highlight the importance of timing, and that customers must act quickly or miss out on the opportunity to participate. Fear is frequently utilised in medical and health marketing to persuade consumers that they must take the medicine or service being given or face the ultimate fear of serious medical problems or even death.

• Advertisements that use the words "fun" and "pleasure" depict customers having a wonderful time and enjoying themselves, all thanks to a product or service. The people in the advertisement are having a wonderful time, and the buyer is lead to assume that they, too, would have a good time if they buy the product or service. Beer, amusement parks, cigarettes, and particular types of autos frequently employ the words "fun" and "pleasure" in their advertising.

• Love-themed ads appeal to people who want to provide for and care for their loved ones. Love, like fear, is a strong and primordial emotion that may influence consumer behaviour. These commercials touch into a deep need to offer only the best for the people we care about most in our life, and the things sold are vital to fulfil that urge. Families, pets, infants and moms, and happy couples are common subjects of these advertising. Pampers, Johnson and Johnson, jewellery stores, and pet stores are just a few examples of businesses that employ love.

• Vanity advertisements appeal to a consumer's sense of well-being, pride, significance, and relevance. This advertising is driven by themes like "the latest and best," "you deserve," new fashion trends, and luxury. Because society places a high value on looks and status, advertising may increase brand knowledge, attention, and action by harnessing these themes. Fashion, personal appearance, luxury products, automobiles, and other industries employ vanity frequently.

Colors evoke intense and often contradictory emotions. Others express pleasure, trust, or calm, while others conjure passion, mystery, and coldness. Every hue in an advertising has a particular role in terms of controlling the ad's mood and perception, and consequently its efficacy in eliciting a certain reaction or action. Here are some instances of how each hue may alter an advertisement's mood:

• Passion, energy, strength, love, power, resolve, intensity, rage, and excitement are all associated with the colour red.

• Blue symbolises depth, stability, knowledge, trust, confidence, and relaxation.

• Blue symbolises depth, stability, knowledge, trust, confidence, and relaxation.

• Yellow: vigour, happiness, warmth, focus, irritation, and delight.

• Purple is associated with knowledge, riches, monarchy, power, luxury, magic, power, soothing, and strength.

• Green represents growth, health, harmony, safety, nature, quiet, and rejuvenation.

• Orange: zeal, zeal, zeal, zeal, zeal, zeal, zeal, zeal, ze

• White connotes purity, light, cleanliness, sterility, innocence, spaciousness, coldness, and unfriendliness.

• Black conjures up images of strength, mystery, elegance, evil, grief, and death; it also conjures up images of confidence, serenity, stability, and mystery.

The entire design and success of an advertising campaign is heavily influenced by psychology. Ads may be developed to elicit desired feelings and reactions, eventually driving desirable customer behaviours, by utilising fundamental psychological concepts. Ads may be tailored to certain demographic or psychographic groups, increasing brand memory, awareness, and affinity.

Understanding the human mind and how to use fundamental psychological concepts is essential for effective advertising and branding, and it's one of the reasons Glint has been helping customers expand their businesses for almost two decades.

Marketing vs. Advertising

A corporation pays to get its message in front of a certain audience through advertising. Marketing is far broader: it encompasses not just all parts of advertising, but also the research required to correctly deliver those commercials, price those goods and services competitively, and track the effectiveness of all connected initiatives.

It's also crucial to comprehend the key distinctions between advertising and marketing.

The process of enhancing client awareness of a product is known as advertising. The process of preparing items for awareness is also included in marketing. While there are expenses associated with marketing, they are not as obvious as the costs associated with advertising. Advertising is one of the most expensive aspects of marketing since it involves posting ads and getting the word out.

There are a few more distinctions to take into account:

• Time: Because a marketing plan involves several kinds of brand promotion, including advertising, it takes longer than just advertising.

• Success measurements: Marketing is primarily concerned with increasing customer awareness of a brand, whereas advertising is frequently judged in terms of conversions.

• Procedures: Each procedure is different. Advertising, on the other hand, concentrates on getting the product known to the public, whereas marketing focuses on things like production and research. Advertising focuses on the best method to describe a product to buyers, whereas marketing explores how to connect a product with its target demographic.

• Aspect: Marketing considers factors like as product, pricing, location, people, promotion, and process, whereas advertising is primarily concerned with promotion.

• Length: Marketing goals often take longer to provide results, but advertising can produce results quickly. A corporation may employ a company to accomplish advertising initiatives, such as running sponsored advertisements or updating the material and blogs on their website, and a brand may have a marketing team to constantly assess the entire marketing plan. The entire advertising approach may alter several times, whereas marketing is unlikely to do so.

• Focus: Marketing is frequently concerned with developing a product or service for a certain market, and it is ultimately concerned with raising awareness. Advertising is to capture the public's attention and increase sales.

The brand has total control over the advertising process. With other sorts of marketing, this isn't always the case. Brands, for example, may not always have influence over the public publicity they get. Although it may incorporate sponsored forms, marketing might be considered an organic strategy. It is long-term oriented, implying that the goal is to nurture the consumer until they convert and become loyal.

Even understanding the distinctions between marketing and advertising is a solid start toward developing a successful plan.

For what reason do the Differences Matter?

The contrasts among promoting and publicizing might be insignificant, yet realizing them can assist you with making a compelling showcasing technique. Monitoring the distinctions isn't just significant with regards to technique, yet additionally picking assets. Joining the two techniques can prompt promoting experts being associated with undertakings that don't identify with their qualities. Brands likewise don't have any desire to squander promoting dollars by focusing on some unacceptable deals channel.

As innovation arises further, the contrasts between the two will turn out to be even less conspicuous. More individuals are moving needs from assorted promoting efforts to publicizing strategies. While the most well-known promoting strategies utilized today are computerized, including online media, content, and paid advertisements, there is still some worth in viewing at your showcasing system in general. Moreover, many publicizing strategies today give the best outcomes when consolidated. For instance, natural substance that offers some benefit to clients is helpful. Be that as it may, supported substance might be important to arrive at your clients.

Promoting versus Promoting Strategies

A methodology is a course of making an arrangement with the expectation of accomplishing an objective. In basic terms, brands make showcasing or publicizing procedures to build brand mindfulness or changes. There are a couple of contrasts in promoting as opposed to publicizing methodologies.

Promoting Strategies

Promoting can be arranged into a couple of significant systems, which include:

- Item

Item alludes to the item you're selling. Items should fulfill shopper need. It very well may be useful to check out why your item is interesting to other comparative items or brands on the lookout. This will assist you with picking which promoting strategies to utilize. Item centers around things like:

- Functionality

- Appearance

- Warranty

- Quality

- Packaging

- Cost

Building up the right cost is likewise significant. Brands need to consider things like apparent worth and opportunity costs. You will likewise factor underway expense and the expense of advertising. Cost centers around:

- Selling cost

- Available limits

- Payment changes

- Price coordinating

- Credit terms

Advancement

Advancement is the most common way of transferring informing or data about your items or administrations. It centers around questions like "What is the best technique to arrive at your clients?" "What data do you want to get across to them in the showcasing strategy that you pick?" Promotion is a sort of publicizing. Advancement centers around the accompanying:

- Sponsorships

- Advertising

- Public relations

- Messaging

- Media

Spot

Spot alludes to supply, or where the item comes from. It is the most common way of picking a circulation, considering diversifying, or it may allude to actual retail or online business. It is the most common way of guaranteeing the client can track down an item. Spot centers around the accompanying:

- Distribution channels

- Logistics strategies

- Service levels

- Location of item

- Market inclusion

Individuals

Individuals alludes to the representatives that make the business run productively. Client care is frequently a major piece of this methodology. Individuals centers around things like:

- Services gave

- The mentality of the brand

- Customer administration

- The appearance of the brand

- Employee depiction

This is additionally alluded to as the five Ps of showcasing. They are components that brands or entrepreneurs control to expand worth and contrast their rivals.

Promoting Strategies

Promoting techniques normally revolve around the objective of receiving the message out in the best way conceivable. The following are a couple of publicizing systems:

Enthusiastic Appeal

Many promoting procedures utilize an enthusiastic allure approach. This implies that the brand endeavors to actuate the passionate reactions of its likely clients. This may incorporate feelings like:

- Anger

- Fear

- Happiness

- A want to further develop looks

Limited time Advertising

Limited time publicizing is a system that basically utilizes advancements to draw in clients. By offering limits or free things, the brand urges the client to attempt the item. Special promoting may incorporate things like:

- Buy one get one free deal

- Discount off your next request coupon

- Promotional cash

- Half off an item

Family-Friendly Messaging

Many brands likewise center around a family-accommodating message. This permits them to arrive at guardians or families with kids to sell an item. Family-accommodating informing might incorporate things like:

- Advertising the security provisions of a vehicle

- Highlighting the pleasant components of a youngster's toy

- Providing guardians with a game that helps with instructive objectives

- Highlighting family includes that will assist families with keeping a bustling timetable

Realities and Statistics

Realities and measurements are other normal strategies for publicizing. Brands furnish clients with realities and insights that urge them to make a move. This may incorporate things like:

- An advertisement that advances familiarity with the adequacy of an item

- A flyer that procures client trust utilizing measurements

- A certificate or rating on an item

- An advertisement that features the factual prevalence of the brand

Since it is becoming simpler for brands to get showcasing messages out to clients, they are met with more commotion. This implies it is harder to stand apart from other brand informing. Furthermore, understanding bulletins or survey advertisements on TV doesn't have the very impact that they once did. Indeed, even clients via web-based media are more particular with regards to which brands they use and culminating your methodology is significant.

How advertising works

Organizations and purchasers the same are hoping to work on their personal satisfaction and proficiency of their business. While a little piece of the populace might have weaknesses that publicizing gains by, I accept that is insignificant. As I would see it, most of organization advertising and staggered promoting endeavors work in this field. Have you at any point been welcome to one of these occasions? They're huge festivals of cheerful individuals marched around the stage with guarantees of large checks, relaxes and even vehicles to convince the visitors to contribute and start selling for them. Vemma, a caffeinated drink MLM, was as of late briefly shut down as a fraudulent business model.

While that is outrageous, it's not the standard. Watch a normal Apple promotion and you will not see limiting and pyramid schemes. All things being equal, you'll watch accounts of individuals releasing their inward imagination using Apple

Gadgets and programming as the apparatuses. Notice Coca-Cola's publicizing and you'll see an attention on the occasions and settings they promote at, attempting to construct brand mindfulness where glad recollections occur. Of later, they've likewise needed to deal with the impression of sweet beverages and the wellbeing hazards that emerge.

Some publicizing chips away at the inspiration to set aside cash (limits), however there are numerous different justifications for why promoting works:

•   Vicinity – Sometimes publicizing is just important to furnish a local crowd with the way that you have an area close by. Maybe you're looking for NY style pizza close by, thus a neighborhood pizza joint publicizes for area put together terms with respect to look or focuses on an interest in pizza inside a sweep around their café.

•	Responsibility – More and more shoppers are giving cautious consideration to organizations that are zeroing in on manageability, variety, and local area inclusion. Promoting can assume a critical part in changing the impression of a nondescript, gigantic company into one that is giving awards and grants to help nearby networks. Salesforce as of late took on a neighbourhood school in Indianapolis, giving $50,000 in hardware to help them.

•	Research – Where do you go when you're exploring your next excursion, your next car buy, your protection, or other significant cost? Promoting educational substance to assist with instructing shoppers and organizations has detonated as of late. While the objective is to assemble trust and authority by giving the fundamental examination, it's not generally the ultimate objective of a buy. Commonly it's giving essential or auxiliary examination that is broadly shared. I frequently see promotions about content that might bear some significance with my companions and send it to them.

•   Emotion – Storytelling has leaped to the front line of many promoting approaches since it not just interfaces sincerely with the crowd, it's additionally created to lead the watcher or peruser through the story. Some might consider this control, however that is vague to a successful promotion that inspires feeling.

•   Persuasion – Utilizing feeling, promoting is frequently powerful. Dr. Robert Cialdini depicts six all inclusive standards of influence that have been logically demonstrated to convince the publicizing crowd – correspondence, shortage, authority, consistency, enjoying and agreement.

Furthermore, Let's Not Forget

In the event that the abhorrent objective of publicizing was to propel a deal, by far most doesn't work by any means. In case promoting were that evil and manipulative, we'd be generally hurrying to McDonalds to invest energy with family and a case of McNuggets! Publicizing is costly and, generally, is a to change insights and increment mindfulness. Promoting, in the same way as other showcasing systems, is a drawn out procedure that has a lot of hazard related with it.

Diverse Advertising tools utilized in industry

Tools/Devices for publicizing assist you with drawing in the most thoughtfulness regarding your independent venture and arrive at the biggest number of conceivably new and bringing customers back. Notwithstanding print, TV and radio, utilize other contemporary instruments to upgrade your advertisement crusade. Contingent upon your financial plan impediments, you can use as not many as a couple of publicizing devices and increment your choices from that point. In the event that fundamental, utilize a time of experimentation to pass judgment on the devices best in making more business and, in this manner, higher benefits.

Web

The Internet has turned into the device of decision for publicizing. Through this adaptable apparatus, market your business utilizing online media locales and mass email administrations. One of the best and most economical publicizing devices related with the Internet is your own site. Change your business site content whenever to cause to notice at least one parts of your business, to feature forthcoming deals or to educate clients concerning significant declarations.

Mobile phone

A convincing promoting device is the PDA. There are numerous applications now accessible that can be transferred to a cell phone that you can use to draw clients. For instance, you may have a major deal on a specific car part. Your Internet and print promoting can show an image that, when checked by possible clients' telephones, furnishes them with a coupon they would then be able to bring to your shop for extra limits. You can utilize comparable applications to illuminate individuals about your area or give other business data.

Verbal Communication

Verbal exchange has been demonstrated to be one of the best instruments for promoting. To work with "getting the news out" about your business, don't think little of the force of your organization's most important promoting instrument: your representatives. They can be your business' diplomats, advancing extraordinary deals and enlisting new clients. With a little training from you, your representatives will actually want to effectively execute the wide range of various promotion instruments available to you.

Computerized/Digital Advertising

Computerized publicizing is the act of conveying limited time content to clients through different on the web and advanced channels.

Advanced publicizing use mediums like web-based media, email, web search tools, portable applications, partner projects and sites to show promotions and messages to crowds.

Conventional (non-advanced) promoting generally followed the shower and ask approach. It connected with the majority, yet the ROI was generally undeterminable. Computerized promoting, as far as we might be concerned today, is intensely information driven and can give you minute subtleties of your missions and results. The accessibility of client information and rich focusing on abilities makes computerized promoting a significant apparatus for organizations to interface with their crowd. It is valuable to recollect that while the associated world offers may ways of coming to and draw in with clients, there is a differentiation between ways that are free or 'natural' and paid or 'inorganic'. Computerized promoting is an 'inorganic' way of coming to and draw in with clients and possibilities.

How Did Digital Advertising Begin?

On October 27th, 1994, one of the main standard advertisements showed up on HotWired.com (Wired Magazine's first site), and the promoting business saw the development of computerized publicizing. The pennant promotion was 468*60 px in size and read "Have you at any point clicked your mouse here? YOU WILL."

The advertisement was for AT&T's virtual visit through seven of the world's craft historical centers. As per Joe McCambley, who dealt with this promotion, it got an incredible 44 percent CTR!

With the arrival of Google AdWords in 2000, Google AdSense in 2003 and Facebook advertisements in 2007, the computerized publicizing industry developed huge amounts at a time. Following, improving and controlling promotions became feasible for little and medium-sized entrepreneurs.

In 2019, computerized publicizing is utilized to direct people to sites, create drives, construct brand mindfulness, set up idea administration, assemble drew in networks and produce deals.

What Are the Digital Advertising Formats?

Since its commencement in 1994, computerized publicizing has been consistently improved upon. Today the different computerized publicizing scene comprises of different promotion designs. You could even utilize a mixture of two advertisement classifications to make another one. For instance, you can utilize remarketing with show advertisements to contact your current guests to remind them to finish a buy. This segment records five of the most regularly utilized computerized advertisement designs.

1. Web index Marketing

While looking for something on Google or Bing, a couple of indexed lists with the tag 'Promotion' show up at the highest point of the Search Engine

Results Page (SERP). These promotions are the aftereffect of web index showcasing.

Web crawler Marketing (SEM) is apparently the most generally utilized advertisement design. In SEM, you bid on watchwords alongside your rivals to show up at the highest point of the page.

2. Show Ads

Promotions, as far as we might be concerned, started here. Show promotions basically use text and pictures and show up on outsider sites, which are normally subsidiary with web crawlers or other advertisement organizations. Numerous sites self-have show promotions too. The most well-known sorts of show promotions are pictures, versatile, text, flags, pop-ups and video advertisements.

3. Web-based Media Ads

Your crowd invests a great deal of energy in web-based media, and this presents an enormous chance to promote your image. You can utilize web-based media stages like Facebook, Twitter, YouTube, Instagram, LinkedIn, Reddit, and so on to advance your image and items. Online media advertisements can assist you with correcting from building a local area, producing leads and expanding occasion participants, to helping site changes, application establishments and developing footfalls to your retail location.

4. Local Advertising

Local advertisements can show up via online media destinations or other website pages, and they don't look like normal promotions. They show up under 'Suggested Reading', 'Related Stories' or 'Advanced Stories' that outwardly match the substance you're right now perusing, just after clicking, you're diverted to the publicist's site. Local promoting is for the most part steered through content disclosure sites like Taboola, Outbrain and Columbia to give some examples.

5. Remarketing

Have you at any point actually look at an item on Amazon and later while looking through your online media feed run over a promotion for that accurate item? That is remarketing. **Also known as retargeting, remarketing utilizes treats to follow you on the web. Pretty much every significant online media stage just as Google right now offer the remarketing highlight.

Sales Promotions in Advertising

Sales Promotion is one of the centre components of the advancement blend. To assemble enduring associations with clients, you really want to discover the kinds of deals that work with your ideal interest group. Simultaneously, you ought to give clients esteem that is comparative with your main subject area.

Advantages of Sales promotion

•   It assists with producing new leads. Deals advancement can support your item picture since it energizes sharing data about it inside gatherings of people identified with your business. If you sell preparing football shoes, individuals enthused about playing football will share the message.

•   Allows reconnecting with your current crowd. When an individual preferred a brand's email pamphlets, they will get customary deals advancements. It is a way of keeping the crowd drew in and keep a nearby association with the organization, which is essential for building devotion.

•	Skyrockets income. Sales Promotion assist organizations with expanding the quantity of sold merchandise, despite the fact that they need to bring down the cost to accomplish that objective. Obviously, just lessening the cost isn't sufficient, individuals should require your item, while the rebate is just one more motivation to make a buy.

•	Increases brand mindfulness. Sales Promotion is a way of making a name for your image since individuals are bound to discuss a company that proposes advantages and sets aside their cash. That is the thing that business advancement does

Sales Promotion Objectives

The primary objective of Sales Promotion is to build interest in a specific item, you can arrive at a few significant objectives. Understanding them will assist you with making a viable advancement technique.

1.   Launch another item. In case you will grow and transform your little bistro into a bread kitchen, you want to arrive at new market portions. You can draw in new clients by offering a free treat with some espresso or propose guests set their own cost now and again.

2.   Attract new customers. This goal ought to be your drawn out objective since it permits your business to develop. Your potential customers are reasonable your rivals' clients, so breaking down their item and advantages, you can offer something more important.

3. Stay cutthroat. Investigating and examining your rivals won't just assist you with drawing in new customers however continually work on your item and client care.

4. Make existing clients purchase more. It's consistently more straightforward to make a current client purchase more than draw in new customers. Give every customer a customized approach — it will assist you with building client dependability. Thus, customers will advance your image naturally.

5. Sell during the slow time of year. Products like swimwear, boats, tents, climate control systems, fridges are certainly more famous in summer however you ought to think about unique methodologies to sell them consistently. Offer time-restricted limits, "1+1=3" crusades, and other showcasing stunts.

6.   Run leeway crusades. They're particularly famous before summer and winter. As vendors need to account for another assortment, they regularly run all out freedom crusades when clients can purchase products from old assortments at incredibly scaled down costs.

Sales Promotion Strategies

Sales Promotion techniques can be isolated into three wide sorts. These are –

•   Pull Strategy – The draw methodology endeavors to get the clients to 'pull' the items from the organization. It includes utilizing advertising correspondence and drives like occasional limits, monetary plans, and so forth

•	Push Strategy – The push procedure endeavours to promote the item away from the organization to the clients. It includes persuading the go-between channels to promote the item from the circulation channels to the last shoppers utilizing limited time and individual selling endeavours. This system includes utilizing strategies grew particularly for affiliates, traders, vendors, merchants, and specialists.

•	Hybrid Strategy – A half breed deals advancement technique utilizes both the force and push system to sell the item with the least obstruction conceivable. It includes drawing in the clients utilizing unique coupons and furthermore giving motivating forces to the shippers to sell the brand's items.

Consumer Sales Promotion

At the point when the business advancement systems are focused on to the end customers, it is alluded to as buyer deals advancement. A model would offer 20% off on specific items to the clients. The fundamental intention of buyer arranged advancement is to build deals straight by drawing in new clients and charming existing ones.

Consumer Sales Promotion Techniques Targeted To Consumers.

Consumer Sales apparatuses utilized for shopper situated advancement are –

• Free Samples: Distributing free examples expands brand mindfulness and triggers the brain science of possession where the individual picks the advanced item if he loved the example.

•   Free Gifts – Offering unconditional presents draw in clients as they get more while paying for less.

•   Discounts/Discount Coupons – Discount coupons are an extraordinary strategy for expanding deals for the present moment. Individuals go for rebate coupons as they let them purchase the items they couldn't manage in any case.

•   Exchange Schemes – Exchange plans draw in numerous clients as they get some worth in any event, for their old item.

•   Finance Schemes – Finance plans like no-cost EMI, low-interest EMI, and so forth makes it more straightforward for clients to buy costly items.

- Shipping Schemes – Sometimes tremendous delivery costs deter the clients from purchasing items. Such momentary delivery plans eliminate rubbing.

- Bundle Discounts – These arrangements are an incredible way of diminishing unsold stock. It incorporates selling packaged items at a cost lesser than when those number of items are purchased independently.

- Bulk Purchase Deals – This is an extraordinary deals advancement strategy to decrease unsold stock. It incorporates giving rebate to clients who purchase in mass.

Trade Sales Promotion

At the point when the advancement exercises are planned remembering the sellers, wholesalers, or specialists, it is called exchange deals advancement. In this sort of deals advancement, offers are furnished inside the exchange channels with a mean to charm retailers, wholesalers, specialists, or merchants. This is done to get more rack space when contrasted with contenders, spur the vendors to sell a greater amount of the brand's items and to build the deals by implication.

Trade Sales Promotion Techniques Targeted To Traders.

• Point Of Purchase Displays – This incorporates giving free place to checkout (POP) show units to the retailers to expand their deals.

• Trade Shows – Trade shows are an incredible deals advancement methodology where the business elevates its item to huge number of merchants in the career expo. Expos likewise witness enormous limits when contrasted with when purchased typically.

• Push Money – Also known as spiffs, this method incorporates additional installments to brokers to persuade them to meet determined objectives. For instance, giving them a $50 reward for each unit for selling item An and $30 for selling item B for a predetermined time frame period.

•	Deal Loaders – These are the gifts given to the brokers (wholesalers and retailers) for requesting a specific amount of item.

•	Trade Deals – These are uncommon concessions given to the traders to urge them to advance a particular item and increment its deals temporarily period.

•	Buying Allowances – Special limits gave to the venders when they request a predetermined number of items.

Sales Promotion Examples

An item can be advanced temporarily utilizing endless strategies. The following are a couple of instances of deals advancement strategies that exist –

The day after Thanksgiving Sale

The day after Thanksgiving deal is an occasional deal which happens just one time per year. It includes enormous limits and extraordinary offers which are restricted to a day. Thus, it expands the business complex.

Buy One Get One

Buy One Get One (BOGO) is a famous sort of sales promotions where two items are presented at a cost of one. This works extraordinary to advance another item or clear the stock toward the finish of the period.

Reference Bonuses

Reference advertising is an incredible deals advancement methodology where the organization pushes its own clients to acquire new clients. This is finished by giving them exceptional limits, offers, cashback, or genuine financial advantages.

Congratulations for completing this Book with your rigorous attention!

You are highly requested to leave a Review about this book that will inspire me to write more books about this particular topic in future.

www.ingramcontent.com/pod-product-compliance
Lightning Source LLC
Chambersburg PA
CBHW052128150726
48002CB00006B/2526